IMAGES
of America

SCOTS OF CHICAGO'S NORTH SHORE

Pres. Woodrow Wilson, who was Scottish on both sides of his family tree, once said, "Every line of strength in American history is a line colored with Scottish blood."

ON THE COVER: Local students of dance instructor "Professor" John Dewar pose for a photo before the third annual Highland dance recital, which was held on February 20, 1923, in the Winnetka Community House. Pictured from left to right are Marilyn Kelley, Edith Campbell, Jean MacKenzie, Joan Harding, Olive Hartshorne, and Marjorie Cable. Instructor John Farquarson Dewar was born in Illinois in 1887 to Scottish immigrant parents. He served his country during World War I. After the war, Dewar was a sugar broker by trade and taught dance as a hobby. Marilyn Kelley and Joan Kelley were granddaughters of Alex and Martha Kelley of Lake Forest. Marilyn and Joan also lived in Lake Forest and attended Highland dance classes, which were held in a hall at nearby Fort Sheridan. Alex Kelley had brought two loads of Aberdeen Angus cattle to Lake Forest for fellow Scotsmen James Anderson and George Findlay. During his second voyage to the United States, the boat on which Alex and his cattle traveled was trapped by ice for several weeks on the Saint Lawrence Seaway. After the long journey, Alex decided not to return to Scotland and make Lake Forest his permanent home.

IMAGES
of America
SCOTS OF CHICAGO'S
NORTH SHORE

David Forlow and Wayne Rethford
Foreword by Gus Noble

ARCADIA
PUBLISHING

Copyright © 2020 by David Forlow and Wayne Rethford
ISBN 978-1-4671-0430-2

Published by Arcadia Publishing
Charleston, South Carolina

Printed in the United States of America

Library of Congress Control Number: 2019951555

For all general information, please contact Arcadia Publishing:
Telephone 843-853-2070
Fax 843-853-0044
E-mail sales@arcadiapublishing.com
For customer service and orders:
Toll-Free 1-888-313-2665

Visit us on the Internet at www.arcadiapublishing.com

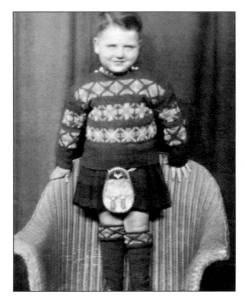

In memory of Mary Ellen (McDonough) Rethford
and John Kelly Forlow (pictured).

"My father came from a very old country in the north and far away,
and he belonged to an old strange race, the race older than any
other. He did not talk of his country but he sang bits of old songs
with words that he said no one could understand anymore."

—Andrew MacLeish

CONTENTS

Foreword

In 1845, immigrant Scots gathered in a burgeoning village of 12,000 residents called Chicago. They formed Illinois's first and still oldest charity, the Illinois St. Andrew Society (also known as "Chicago Scots"). Their purpose was simple: to "relieve the distressed." Almost 175 years later, our mission remains much the same. We nourish Scottish identity through service, fellowship, and celebration of Scottish culture. Around the world, there are many societies that celebrate Scotland's culture, but there is only one that has developed an elder-care community as a defined charitable purpose. For more than 100 years, we have made good on our commitment to serve seniors at Caledonia Senior Living, a beautiful five-acre campus nestled in the forest preserve, just west of downtown Chicago.

The Chicago Scots also reach out to the next generation by providing scholarships to students in Scotland and the USA. We host events like the Scottish Festival and Highland Games to educate, entertain, and promote Scottish culture. We organize initiatives like the Scottish History Forum, Scottish Genealogy Society, and the world's only Scottish American Museum and Hall of Fame to tell the stories of Scottish journeys to and experiences in North America. The Chicago Scots welcome everyone who is Scottish by birth, by heritage, or simply by inclination.

If someone is far from home, or can no longer live at home on their own, they long for a sense of connection, of calm, of coming home. The Chicago Scots provide those nourishing bonds to culture care and community for all.

I am most grateful to my friends and fellow Scots, Wayne Rethford, and David Forlow for putting this book together. I hope that reading this book brings you, just as it brought me, feelings of great Scottish pride and admiration for the contributions and accomplishments of the early Scots.

—Gus Noble
President, Chicago Scots

ACKNOWLEDGMENTS

The tradition in the Highlands of Scotland required that when a visitor in need arrived on your doorstep, they were to be welcomed without question. This tradition of Scots helping Scots is alive and well, and it was never more apparent as the authors conducted their research for this book. Dozens of families from around the globe shared family photographs and information—far too many to mention in this space. Packages with family photographs arrived from as far away as Australia. The contribution of Elaine Rethford was invaluable, as she hunted down information, fact-checked, and searched through the Scottish-American History Museum collection. (Unless otherwise noted, all images courtesy the Scottish-American History Museum.) Laurie Stein, curator at the History Center of Lake Forest–Lake Bluff, always patiently fielded never-ending requests for information and photographs (indicated by LFLBHS). The collection and interactive displays in the History Center at 509 East Deerpath in Lake Forest are well worth the trip. The staff at the Lake Bluff History Museum were another great resource. Shirley McDonald Paddock and Art Miller are two local Lake Forest history experts who, from the very beginning, kindly shared their knowledge. Nancy Webster, at the Highland Park Historical Society, helped track down information about the many Scots who lived and worked in Highland Park. Jennifer Durot and the Historic Millburn Community Association were very helpful. Stephen Jacobs, in the Lake Forest Library Media Center, provided lots of guidance. Last but not least, Molly Forlow spent hours proofreading and very patiently listened to a nonstop litany of local Scottish history.

Was Like Us!

INTRODUCTION

Centuries of battling invaders—from Romans to Vikings, to the "Auld Enemy," the English—imbued Scots with a fiercely independent streak. Scots also had an early educational advantage. In 1616, the Scottish Parliament required every parish to establish a school to be run by local elected officials. Education made it possible for even the poorest Scottish children to improve their lot in life. Access to Scottish universities was also more open than in most of Europe. Scots soon grew to view education, self-determination, and religious freedom as rights and bristled when outsiders tried to impose their will.

Beginning in the early 1600s, nearly 500,000 mostly Protestant Scots moved into Northern Ireland in what is called the Plantation of Ulster. But Scots in both Ulster and Scotland found themselves under continued pressure to conform their beliefs. By the mid-1700s, almost 750,000 Scots left Ulster and Scotland for North America. Scots in the New World were eager to help their countrymen. In 1729, they formed a St. Andrew Society in Charleston, South Carolina. The St. Andrew Society of Philadelphia was formed in 1747, and five members would become signers of the Declaration of Independence. The St. Andrew Society of New York was founded in 1756, and three of its members signed the Declaration of Independence. When President Bush proclaimed April 6 as National Tartan Day, researchers noted that nearly half the signatories of the Declaration of Independence were of Scottish ancestry. Thirty-five of the generals serving under Washington were Scots, as were three out of four members of his cabinet. Three out of five of the judges on the first Supreme Court were Scots as well.

By 1758, Scottish Highland soldiers had pressed west as far as the Ohio River Valley. In 1765, the 42nd Scottish Highlander Regiment of the Black Watch marched to the Mississippi and took control in the name of the British Crown. Trading posts were established, and Scots followed. One of those was John Kinzie, who came to be called the Father of Chicago. He was born John MacKenzie Jr. in Quebec. John Sr. was born in Scotland and served as a surgeon in the British Army. After training as a silversmith, John Jr. decided to become a fur trader in Michigan, where he befriended the local Native Americans and learned their language. They called him Shawneeawkee, or Silver Man. Around this time, he changed his name to Kinzie. It is thought he did this so to better blend between various trading partners who were often at odds with one another. Around 1800, John Kinzie married Eleanor McKillip (who was of Scottish descent). They lived in a cabin along the Chicago River and became the first permanent white settlers. Three children were born to John and Eleanor in Chicago: daughters Ellen and Maria and son Robert. Kinzie was appointed the first justice of the peace of the newly created territory. When the Potawatomi attacked Fort Dearborn in 1812, the Kinzie family were spared because of their friendship with Chief Sauganash, who was born Thomas "Billy" Caldwell to a Potawatomi mother and William Caldwell, an Ulster-Scots immigrant father.

Scotsman David McKee arrived in Chicago in 1822 and became the village's first blacksmith, and shortly after, Alexander Raffen of Cupar, Scotland, became Chicago's first plumber. The

Duncan Act of 1824 called for the establishment of free schools in Illinois. The Duncan family was from Kirkcudbright, Scotland. Scotsman Stephen Forbes opened Chicago's first school in 1830. The population of Chicago reached 200 in the year 1833. The Treaty of Chicago and then the Potawatomi Indian Treaty opened northern Illinois to settlers. Chief Chechequay and Chief Sauganash helped negotiate on behalf of the Native Americans. Chechequay's birth name was Alexander Robinson. He was born to an Ulster-Scots father and Ottawa mother. So, it was two Scots who cleared the path for settlers in northern Illinois.

George Smith from Old Deer, Scotland, arrived in Chicago in 1834 just as the population reached 400. He invested in land as far north as Wisconsin and made a fortune. Along with other Scottish investors, Smith created the Illinois Investment Company. Scottish partners Alexander Anderson, Patrick Strachan, W.D. Scott, and Alexander Mitchell joined Smith, and in 1839, they were granted a charter for the first bank in Illinois and Wisconsin. The bank issued its own currency, which was used by all of the large canal contractors to pay employees. The leading canal builders at the time were George Steele, George Barnet, George Armour, and Robert Milne—all Scottish born.

George Steel and George Armour became partners and built much of the Illinois and Michigan Canal as well as portions of the Chicago, Burlington & Quincy Railroad. They continued to use currency printed by George Smith's bank. Subsequent members of the Steele and Armour families would move into Lake County and play significant roles in the founding of Lake Forest. Scots-born Sylvester Lind worked for George Smith and later served more terms as Lake Forest mayor than any other. The first postmaster in present-day Highland Park, Lake Forest, and Libertyville were all Steele's.

In 1845, when Chicago was still a small town, Scots established the Illinois St. Andrew Society. George Steele was its first president. From its very beginning more than 175 years ago, the Illinois St. Andrew Society has had a simple but important mission "relieve the distressed." The 1846 Potato Famine prompted another wave of immigrants. More than 80 percent of the crop in Ireland and Scotland was lost. Upward of one million Irish died from starvation and related disease. Despite the fact that four-fifths of the Scottish Highlander's diet was potatoes, in Scotland, fewer than 1,000 died. Scots were well-organized, and aid poured in from around the world, including food shipments from Chicago. Landlords in the Highlands soon discovered that raising sheep was far more profitable than renting to tenant farmers. Thousands of Scots were evicted in what is called "the Clearances." Some Scots had no choice but to accept indentured work agreements to cover the cost of emigration. Life was just as difficult in crowded Scottish cities. In 1880, over half of all the deaths in Glasgow were children under the age of 10. During the 1800s, over one million Scots left their homeland, and thousands came to Illinois.

These Scottish immigrants left an indelible mark on the Chicagoland area. Philip Armour funded the Armour Institute, which today is the Illinois Institute of Technology. Gifts from Stephen Douglas, John Crerar, and Andrew MacLeish helped found the University of Chicago. McCormick Place and McCormick Seminary are named for the Scottish family who founded International Harvester as well as the *Chicago Tribune*. Several buildings at Northwestern University are named for Scots, including McGaw Hall. Scots helped found both Lake Forest and Lake Forest College. Scots founded businesses such as Carson, Pirie and Scott, and Quaker Oats. Today, we still see many Scottish place names like Bannockburn, Dundee, Elgin, Glencoe, and Inverness, to name just a few. In the pages that follow, the authors tell just a few of these Scottish stories.

Murrie Blacksmith on Deerpath Road in Lake Forest in 1908. At the far left is William Heaney, the son of a Scot and a coachman for the Pirie family, who originated in Errol, Scotland. Third and fourth from left is John and Ellen Gault, respectively, from Aberdeenshire. In the center are members of the Murrie family from Perthshire. On the far right is the coachman for the Armour family, who originated in Ayrshire. The Scottish born Murrie family were area pioneers, arriving in Lake County before 1850. James Murrie was an early justice of the peace, and John Murrie worked for fellow Scot James Anderson in his Lake Forest General Store. Allen Murrie operated his blacksmith shop on Deerpath Road in Lake Forest, where he employed several other Scots. His daughter Helen worked as a stenographer. As a teenager, son Clifford worked as a farm laborer while the youngest son, Richard, worked at a dry-cleaning store. Clifford and Richard went on to open Murrie Dry Cleaning. They operated a store on Western Avenue in Lake Forest and another on Scranton Avenue in Lake Bluff; both buildings were designed by Stanley Anderson, grandson of James Anderson.

One

EARLIEST SETTLERS
AND LAKE FOREST

1 JOHN DEAN.   2 J. BAPTISTE BEAUBIEN.   3 FORT DEARBORN.   4 Dr WOLCOTT.   5 JOHN KINZIE.

CHICAGO IN 1831.

PUBLISHED BY RUFUS BLANCHARD, 132 CLARK ST.

The John Kinzie home near Fort Dearborn is seen here in Chicago. Kinzie is sometimes called "the Father of Chicago." He was born in Quebec around 1763 to John and Anne MacKenzie. John Sr. was born in Scotland and was a surgeon in the British army. It is surmised that John Jr. adopted the name "Kinzie" to more easily blend between the nationalities of his various trading partners. (Library of Congress.)

James Hay Simpson (top left) and family are pictured here around 1890. Robert Simpson and Rose Lawson were married in Scotland and came to the United States in 1838 with their six children, including son James. Two more children were born in Lake County. Several other Scottish families had settled in the area, including the Bell, Duncan, Kennedy, MacIntyre, Lawson, Pope, and Steele families. (Bill Vanderpool.)

Mary Ellen Simpson was the daughter of Robert and Mary Simpson Jr. She was born in Evanston in 1873 and married George Anderson in 1903. George was born in 1872, the son of James Anderson from Scotland. The couple owned a home on Vine Avenue in Lake Forest. (James Anderson and Company.)

James Steele was born in Scotland in 1818 and was among the earliest settlers in Lake County. By 1845, Scots in Chicago established the Illinois St. Andrew Society, with George Steele as the first president. William Steele and his four sons were among the very first settling on land that today is west Lake Forest along present-day Waukegan Road. (Bill Vanderpool.)

Ellen Simpson was born in Keith, Scotland. In 1848, Ellen married James Steele in Shields Township. More than 25 children were born to the various Steele families who lived in Lake County. Andrew Steele served as the first Lake Forest postmaster. The first postmaster of Highland Park and Libertyville were also Steele's. Descendants of these families would live in Lake Forest for the next 100 years. (Bill Vanderpool.)

Around 1855, Presbyterians decided they should build a school in the country. Led by Pastor Robert Patterson, an Ulster Scot, a group boarded a train and convinced the conductor to stop just south of the present-day East Lake Forest train station. As they stood among the trees overlooking Lake Michigan, one pointed at the lake and then the trees, and the name "Lake Forest" was chosen. (Lake Forest College.)

Andrew Carnegie was born in Dunfermline, Scotland, in 1835 and was a member of the New York St. Andrew's Society. Carnegie became personal friends with Lake Forest College president Rev. Robert Patterson. Carnegie Hall at Lake Forest College was funded by Andrew. Carnegie built more than 100 libraries in Illinois, including libraries in Wilmette, Waukegan, Park Ridge, Highland Park, Evanston, and Des Plaines.

Sylvester Lind was born in 1808 in Tarves, Scotland. He worked as a currier for "Silent" George Smith, the Scotsman who formed the first bank in Chicago and made trips between Chicago and Wisconsin. In 1856, the Lake Forest Association was formed, and Lind was named the first trustee. Lind was the first of many from the Aberdeenshire area who settled in Lake Forest.

Lind later made a fortune in the lumber business and owned a full business block in Chicago. He pledged $100,000 to have a school built in Lake Forest, so Lind University was chartered in 1857. Unfortunately, as a result of a financial panic, Lind was unable to meet his pledge. The name of the school was changed to Lake Forest University.

Sylvester Lind recovered financially and built a large house on Deerpath in Lake Forest. Information in the Lake Forest College collection says the Lind home served as a stop on the Underground Railway. Lind was a staunch abolitionist, often using his lumber boats to help escaped slaves reach freedom in Canada. Lind served more terms than any other Lake Forest Mayor. (HCLFLB.)

The Illinois Highland Guard was commanded by John McArthur, who served as president of the Illinois St. Andrew Society. The group was organized in 1856 and met in the Sylvester Lind building. During the Civil War, they sustained heavy losses at Shiloh and Corinth. On October 5, 1864, alone, they lost 57 of the remaining 161 men. Survivors marched to the sea with General Sherman. (*Military History Matters.*)

In 1851, James Anderson left Aberdeenshire, Scotland. He secured a job clearing land in Lake Forest in exchange for the small house Sylvester Lind had built. Anderson ran a general store located just west of the present-day Lake Forest train station on Western Avenue. Enterprising James also operated a lumber yard in town and employed many immigrant Scots. (The Anderson family.)

In 1871, Anderson's nephew, George Findlay, arrived in Lake Forest. Six years later, James Anderson and George imported four cows and one bull to Lake Forest, making them the first registered Angus herd in the United States. The Anderson-Findlay operation later supplied cattle to the XIT Ranch in Texas, which stretched over three million acres. George Findlay became the manager of XIT in 1888. (The Anderson family.)

George Findlay returned from Texas in 1903 and opened Lake Forest's first bank in a small building on Deerpath, of which he was president. The majority of the officers were Scots, including two Findlays, an Anderson, and a Steele. In 1907, Lake Forest saw its second bank open, with George Anderson as vice president. Several other Scots were officers, including William Strang, whose sister had married an Anderson. In 1915, the two banks merged and moved to a new building in Lake Forest's Market Square. As a result, the street in front of the building was renamed Bank Lane. Again, Scots dominated the board of the combined bank, with an Armour, Ewing, McElwee, McLennan, Pirie, and a Wilson all serving. (HCLFLB.)

In the early 1900s, the Anderson family built a large commercial building on the corner of Western Avenue and Deerpath. The Anderson Bank and general store operated out of the ground floor with apartments on the upper levels. Today, the ground floor houses a Walgreens. James Anderson Jr. became an engineer and helped survey much of Lake Forest. Almost 125 years later, Anderson and Company is still in business. (HCLFLB.)

James Anderson's grandson Stanley Anderson designed dozens of homes and buildings in the area. Notable among them are Lake Forest High School, Lake Forest Hospital, and many of the buildings, which, today, form downtown Lake Forest. Stanley also designed a house on King Muir Road that was patterned after Greywalls, a hotel on Muirfield Golf Course in Scotland. (The Stanley Anderson Collection.)

In 1878, a 19-year-old, Alexander Kelley, brought a shipment of Anderson- Findlay cattle to Lake Forest that became part of the first registered herd of black Angus cattle in the United States. The journey from Aberdeenshire to Lake Forest took seven weeks. After returning to Scotland and bringing a second shipment of cattle, Kelley decided to make Lake Forest his permanent home. (The Kelley family.)

Alex started a road-building company and employed his sons. By 1923, they had paved over half of the town's streets and driveways, working as far south as Fort Sheridan. When Alex and wife Martha celebrated their 50th anniversary in 1935, all seven of their children (and nearly all their grandchildren) still lived within just a few blocks. (The Kelley family.)

Gordon Kelley was born and raised in Lake Forest. Kelley was stationed at Pearl Harbor when the Japanese attacked. Gordon went on to fly a B-17 Flying Fortress he named "Uncle Biff." Kelley logged more than 6,000 flight hours. He was awarded the Silver Star for Gallantry, the Air Medal, and Distinguished Flying Cross with Oak Leaf Clusters. (The Kelley family.)

At age 20, James King Jr. (holding James III) left Scotland. He accepted a job to deliver a load of Anderson-Findlay cattle to Lake Forest. During a brief layover in Liverpool, James Jr. met his future wife, Helen Gibson, in a bookstore. The next stop was Quebec and then through the Erie Canal, around the Great Lakes, and to Illinois. The total journey took seven weeks. (The King family.)

Four years after James Jr. arrived in the United States, Helen Gibson followed. James met her in New York, and a day later, they were married. The marriage certificate lists James as a farmer. James and Helen made Lake Forest their home. James served on the first Lake Forest Fire Brigade and then as township justice of the peace. He took correspondence courses and was a voracious reader. (The King family.)

In 1897, James King Jr., (seen here with his daughter) became a Lake Forest city clerk, a job he held for the next 38 years, serving under 13 mayors. James retired in 1932 at age 74. Lake Forest awarded this son of an illiterate farmhand a gold star for his faithful service. In Lake Forest, James and Helen raised eight children in their home at 857 North Summit Avenue. (The King family.)

Scottish-born Alex Robertson arrived in Lake Forest in 1883 and his wife, Mary, in 1888. Alex had brought a shipment of Anderson-Findlay Angus cattle. He worked as a clerk in the James Anderson store and eventually owned his own home on Summit Avenue. Sons George and Keith opened a men's clothing store, which even sold kilts. (HCLFLB.)

James Robertson was the younger brother to Alex. James came to Lake Forest in 1893. In 1895, he married Scottish-born Agnes Duncan. James worked as a city sewer builder. Sons Frank and Arthur worked for the Lake Forest Fire Department, Jack was a police officer, and Henry worked for the street department. Robertson family members served Lake Forest for the 100 continuous years. (HCLFLB.)

Alexander and Mary (Simpson) Brebner were both born in Aberdeenshire, Scotland. They were married in 1907 and came to the United States just a few months later. A year after arriving in the United States, Alex Jr. was born. Alex Sr. worked as a gardener on an estate in Lake Forest. Alex Jr., known as "Sandy," became a Lake Forest Police officer. (HCLFLB.)

In 1935, Alexander Brebner Jr. was working as a police officer when he married Adeline Baldwin. The young couple bought a home on Griffith Road. Proud Lake Forest chief of police Alexander Brebner Jr. is pictured sitting in the front-row center. Scots-born James Gordon had served as the first-ever police officer in Lake Forest and worked until the mid-1930s when he was in his 70s. (HCLFLB.)

This is a 1912 image of the Lake Forest Volunteer Fire Department. Early Lake Forest Fire and Police Departments included many Scots: Joseph Anderson, George Anderson, Alex Brebner, Henry Duncan, James Gordon, Harold Griffis, George Kelley, James King, Charles Gunn, William Lawson, Frank Robertson, John Robertson, George Scott, and James Watt. Robertson family members continue to serve as firefighters to this day, racking up a combined 200-plus years of community service. (HCLFLB.)

Charles Russell (in Masonic uniform) was born in Lake Forest in 1870. His father, Robert, from Edinburgh, was an early home builder. Charles became one of the very first students at Lake Forest Academy. Charles went on to study civil engineering at the University of Illinois. He worked as Lake Forest city engineer and plumbing inspector and later held the office of Lake County surveyor. (The Russel family.)

William Gordon moved from Scotland to the United States in 1883. William Gordon found work in Lake Forest as a carpenter. Signe Nelson was born in Sweden, and she moved to the United States a few years after William Gordon. The couple met and married and made their home on Forest Avenue. (The Gordon family.)

William Gordon and wife Signe had three children: Elsie, Ester, and Harold. Tragically, while Signe was pregnant with their fourth child Jane, William fell from a roof and died. Signe made ends meet by working as a laundress and later as a waitress. Son Harold worked as a clerk in the Lake Forest Post Office. (The Gordon family.)

James Gordon (center) came to the United States from Scotland in 1884 and became the first Lake Forest police officer, operating on foot and sometimes bicycle. Scottish-born James Watt was hired as the third-ever Lake Forest police officer. Brother Jack Gordon operated a bicycle store on Western Avenue. After 36 years of service, 70-year-old James Gordon was still working as a police officer. (HCLFLB.)

In 1914, William Gordon and his son William Jr. set sail for Lake Forest. William Sr. listed his occupation as "shoemaker," and William Jr. as "bartender." William Gordon Jr. later moved to Australia, where his grandson organized a famine relief concert in January 1985. The concert was part of the Live Aid concerts, which raised more than $200 million for famine relief in Ethiopia. (William Gordon III.)

The Gunn Grocery Store can be seen on the awning of this early 1900s image taken on Western Avenue in Lake Forest. All fifteen children born to Donald and Margaret Gunn of Caithness, Scotland, left their homeland for the United States, and five came to Lake Forest, where Charles Thomson "CT" Gunn opened a grocery store. CT also served on the first Lake Forest Fire Department. (HCLFLB.)

Grace Gunn (bottom right), daughter of CT Gunn, is seen with her Lake Forest Sunday school class. CT Gunn bought land in Lake Forest from fellow Scot Francis Calvert and built a house on Illinois Road. CT also owned eight acres, which today forms the entrance to Deerpath Golf Club. In 1927, Stanley Anderson designed a new building at 241 Deerpath for the growing grocery business. (The Kelley family.)

John and Ellen Gault married in Aberdeenshire, where daughter Minne was born. The family moved to Lake Forest, where John delivered coal by horse and wagon. Son Jack was born in 1909, but in 1911, Ellen died after a miscarriage. Unable to care for his children by himself, John returned to Scotland and left them with family members. In 1913, John returned to Lake Forest by himself. (The Gault family.)

Joseph Falconer and brother William are pictured around 1914. Joseph was born in Scotland in 1897. During World War I, he enlisted in the British Army. Joseph eventually settled in Lake Forest and married Scottish born Jessie Connon. Their son Joseph Jr. was born in 1928. Joseph Sr. worked as a gardener, and the family lived on Cherry Avenue and later Laurel Avenue in Lake Forest. (The Falconer family.)

Robert Haire (center) from Irvine, Scotland, was fascinated by cars. Robert set sail for the United States and secured work as a chauffeur for the Blair family. In 1927, Robert formed the Chauffeur Benevolent Association and served as president. In Lake Forest, Robert worked for J. Ogden Armour. There were more than a dozen Scottish-born chauffeurs working in Lake Forest at that time. (The Haire family.)

Brothers George and Robert Preston were born in Edinburgh, Scotland, and both immigrated to Lake Forest. George worked for fellow Scot James Anderson as a clerk in his grocery store on Western Avenue. Robert was a gardener, and he lived and worked at the Armour Estate in Lake Bluff–Tangley Oaks. (The Preston family.)

Thomas Sneddon from Kirkcudbright worked for William Clow in Lake Bluff. Two other Sneddon brothers also came to Lake Forest. Frank Sneddon worked as a Chauffeur and lived with Scottish-born Jane and Robert Chalmers on Mayflower Road. Older brother William (above) arrived in Lake Forest from Kirkcudbright 1907 with his wife, Janet, and three daughters. (HCLFLB.)

William Sneddon brought several other Scots to Lake Forest. William McCall and John Edgar lived and worked on the farm. William Burgess also came from Kirkcudbright to work on the farm. Family members say his passage was paid in return for one year of farm labor. Burgess later worked for Standard Oil and bought a house on June Terrace in Lake Forest. (HCLFLB.)

John Martin Littlejohn was born in Glasgow, Scotland, in 1867, where he studied theology, law, medicine, and philosophy. At age 22, his doctor told him he did not have long to live and that he should travel to the United States to extend his life. John went on to study at the American School of Osteopathy in Kirksville, Missouri. (Chicago College of Osteopathic Medicine.)

Littlejohn founded the Littlejohn College and Teaching Hospital in Chicago. In 1911, he bought a house in Lake Bluff from Scottish born William Wallace. There he lived with his wife, Mabel, six children, and his mother. Littlejohn had become connected with the Chautauqua movement and was a speaker at gatherings. In 1917, Littlejohn returned to Great Britain and founded the British School for Osteopathy. (Chicago College of Osteopathic Medicine.)

Neil and Helen Campbell are seen at the Lake Forest wedding of their daughter Jean to Maj. Kenneth Procter. Neil Nelson Campbell was born in Canada in 1885. His father was Dugald Campbell, and his mother Annie McPhee; both families originated in Argyllshire, Scotland. Neil's first job after engineering school was in Lake Forest, working under James Anderson Jr. (The Campbell family.)

Neil and Helen Campbell are pictured with daughter Jean and six-week-old granddaughter Chrissy. The Campbell family had moved to Zion, Illinois, in 1901. After Neil Campbell graduated from the University of Illinois with an engineering degree, he married Helen Fielden in Zion. Neil designed and built a house on Washington Circle in Lake Forest. (The Campbell family.)

In 1955, Neil Campbell traveled to Scotland to visit family. He is seen here with Ian Douglas Campbell, the 11th Duke of Argyle. From 1917 until 1948, Campbell worked as the Lake Forest city engineer and then as Lake Forest city manager until 1955. Campbell served the City of Lake Forest for a total of 38 years. (The Campbell family.)

Alex and Helen (Irons) Kelly are seen here during Alex's retirement ceremony. The Kellys immigrated to Lake Forest in 1923, where they lived at 137 Atteridge Road. Alex was employed as a groundskeeper at the Lake Forest Presbyterian Church and served as church beadle for many years. Helen was a school teacher in Scotland but became a full-time mom to children Joan and George. (HCLFLB.)

In 1872, Rev. Matthew Parkhurst traveled to Scotland, where he met and married Mary Ann Thomson. Daughters Catherine and Jane were born in Scotland. Four additional children were later born in the United States. Parkhurst was a pastor at Grace Methodist Church in Chicago, which was lost in the Great Chicago Fire. Just days later, he preached from the back of a wagon and raised money to immediately rebuild. (The Parkhurst family.)

Catherine Isabella Thomson Parkhurst (bottom left) with her parents and siblings. The family owned a home in Lake Bluff they named Ivy Bank. Catherine was born in Stirling, Scotland, in 1877. In 1920, she married Charles George Simpson of Evanston, the son of Robert Simpson. Robert had come from Scotland and was part of a group of Scottish farming pioneers in Lake County. (The Parkhurst family.)

Charles Blair McDonald completed his studies at St. Andrews University and came to Chicago, where he brought with him a passion for golf. He helped lay out a few holes on the Farwell Estate in Lake Forest. His father had served as president of the Illinois St. Andrew Society. Many refer to Charles as the father of golf in the United States.

Willie Marshall trained in the Forgan golf shop in St. Andrews. He lived next to the Foulis brothers, who designed the Onwentsia golf course in Lake Forest, where Willie became head pro. Willie built the first-ever home on Atteridge Road in Lake Forest and would walk to work. The Marshall family had Scottish neighbors next door: siblings Jack, Murn, and Catherine Millar. (Michael Marshall.)

Alex Pirie was born in St. Andrews in 1876 and lived very near the 18th green of the Old Course. The Pirie home was within two blocks of the Foulis, Forgan, Marshall, and Millar families. All who would later be connected to Lake Forest. Alex came to the United States as a teenager. (Tom Dobbins.)

Alex Pirie lived on Atteridge Road in Lake Forest, just a few doors down from the Marshall family. Proximity must have kindled a spark, as Pirie's daughter Margaret married William Marshall's son James. Pirie's other daughter Grant married Ted Watt, who lived a pitching wedge away on Oakwood. Ted's parents were from Scotland. (Tom Dobbins.)

Alex Pirie designed Deerpath Golf Club in Lake Forest, Glen Flora, in Waukegan and became the first pro at Old Elm Golf Club in Highland Park. Alex served as president of the US Professional Golfers' Association (first row, second from left). As president, he awarded the Ryder Cup in 1931 and has been inducted into the US Golf Hall of Fame. (Tom Dobbins.)

William MacMillan married Ann McIlwraith in Paisley, Scotland, in 1900. William worked as a delivery man for a candy manufacturer. The couple had nine children and moved to Lake Forest in 1928, where William found work for the City of Lake Forest in the streets department. William later took a job with the Chicago & Northwestern Railroad. (The MacMillan family.)

Gordon "Mickey" Cochrane was a Major League Baseball two-time MVP and three-time World Series champion. In 1937, Cochrane was hit in the head by a pitch, which ended his career. During World War II, Cochrane joined the Navy at Great Lakes. After the war, Cochrane lived in Lake Forest and later in Lake Bluff. Cochrane died of cancer when he was just 59 years old.

Gordon Cochrane, father John, and mother Sadie are pictured here. Both sides of Cochrane's family tree were Scottish, but the press dubbed him "Mickey," believing that he was just another Irish "Mick." Cochrane's baseball friends called him "Mike," and his family called him Gordon. Ironically, Yankee Hall of Famer Mickey Mantle was named for him.

Two

Beyond Lake Forest

Robert Fergusson was born in Scotland in 1878. At age 12, he became a cabin boy on a sailing ship. He was intrigued by the ability of fish oil to prevent rust. He moved to Chicago and began selling a rust proofing-product he named Rust-Oleum. Fergusson lived in Wilmette and was an active member of the Illinois St. Andrew Society. (Rust-Oleum Corporation.)

THE LATE ALLAN PINKERTON.

Allan Pinkerton was born in Glasgow, Scotland, where he married Joan Carfrae. The couple immigrated to the United States and settled in Dundee, Illinois, where Pinkerton made beer barrels. Two children were born in Dundee to Allan and Joan, daughter Isabelle, and son William. The Pinkerton home became a "station" on the Underground Railroad. In 1859, Pinkerton attended secret meetings with John Brown and Frederick Douglass. (Library of Congress.)

Pictured from left to right are Allan Pinkerton, President Lincoln, and General McClellan. During the Civil War, Pinkerton was head of the Union Intelligence Service. Pinkerton foiled an assassination plot while guarding Lincoln on the way to his inauguration. The Pinkerton family moved to Chicago, and Allan became Chicago's first detective. He later founded the Pinkerton Detective Agency. Pinkerton continued his involvement with the abolitionist movement. (Library of Congress.)

William Chalmers (pictured) courted Joan Pinkerton, and soon, the couple was engaged. Allan Pinkerton opposed the marriage because he thought William would never amount to much. But William and his Scottish-born father helped found the firm, which became the largest manufacturer of mining machinery in the world. In 1900, they merged and became Allis-Chalmers, with William as president.

Seen here are Joan (Pinkerton) Chalmers and her daughter, also named Joan, around 1884. The Chalmers were known for their philanthropy and supported numerous causes, including the Illinois St. Andrew Society and the Scottish Old Peoples' Home. William Chalmers was the director of the Columbian Exposition and the Field Museum. The family was members of many clubs, including the Saddle and Cycle Club and Lake Geneva Country Club.

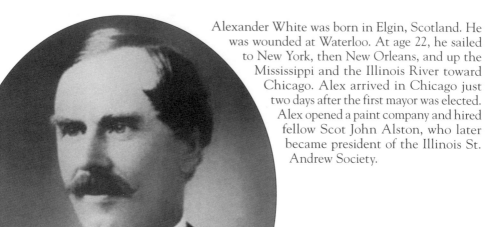

Alexander White was born in Elgin, Scotland. He was wounded at Waterloo. At age 22, he sailed to New York, then New Orleans, and up the Mississippi and the Illinois River toward Chicago. Alex arrived in Chicago just two days after the first mayor was elected. Alex opened a paint company and hired fellow Scot John Alston, who later became president of the Illinois St. Andrew Society.

Alex White expanded his business from paints to real estate. He eventually owned several commercial buildings. The Alexander White Block on Lake Street in Chicago survives to this day. Alex was one of the original trustees of the Lake Forest Association. He purchased the Thompson mansion and gardens, which were described as "perhaps the most beautiful place in Lake Forest."

The Fletcher family was from
Argyll, Scotland. In Highland
Park, Archibald Fletcher ran a large
lumbermill. John Raffen was born
in Cupar, Scotland. His family was
the first plumbers in Chicago. John
joined the California gold rush,
making the journey on foot. He
returned a wealthy man and bought
an iron foundry business. He built a
fine home in Highland Park and took
over the Fletcher lumber business.

John Alston twice served as
president of the Illinois St.
Andrew Society. He was a
prominent manufacturer of
paints in Chicago. Later in
life, he co-owned a lumber
mill in Highland Park. He was
born in Glasgow in 1811 and
died in 1889 at the age of 78.
Mary Lincoln, after the tragic
death of her husband, lived
in Chicago with the Alston
family, who were old friends.

David Erskine was born in Kirkcudbright, Scotland. By 1870, David, wife Harriet, and eight children were living in Waukegan, where David had opened an insurance agency. Son Fred later operated Fred Erskine Insurance, Real Estate and Loans, operated out of 127 North Genesee Street in Waukegan. In 1909, David Erskine Jr. struck out on his own and opened the Erskine Bank in Highland Park. (Highland Park Historical Society.)

At the age of just 22, David Erskine Jr. was named Highland Park justice of the peace. When he was 34, he was elected alderman and, two years later, was elected mayor of Highland Park. David later built the beautiful Erskine Bank Building at 513 Central Avenue, Highland Park. More than 100 years later, the building today serves as the home of Chase Bank.

John Alexander Dowie was born in 1847 in Edinburgh, Scotland, where he studied theology and became a pastor. After spending some time in Australia and San Francisco, he moved to Chicago in 1890. He staged faith healings near the Chicago World's Fair, and his following grew to more than 6,000. In 1900, Reverend Dowie founded the city of Zion, which is 40 miles north of Chicago. His dream was a new utopian society where he hoped followers could work, worship, and recreate without the temptations of the world. Streets were given biblical names, except for two streets named for Dowie's native Scotland: Caledonia Boulevard and Edina Street (which is short for Edinburgh). (Zion Historical Society.)

James Patten was born in 1852 in Illinois. His wife, Amanda Buchanan, was also of Scottish heritage. Patten became a hugely successful grain trader. The family home in Evanston had 15 fireplaces. A newspaper report mentioned a Scottish thistle motif, "which runs all over the Patten house, in stone, wood, brass, and even wallpaper." Patten was elected Evanston mayor in 1901. (Northwestern University Archives.)

Patten was a generous supporter of the Illinois St. Andrew Society. At the time of his death, his estate was valued at more than $20 million. Patten had served as president of the Northwestern University Board of Trustees, and after Amanda Patten passed away, the family home was donated to the school. Patten Gymnasium is named for the family. (Northwestern University Archives.)

William Kelly was born in Hamilton, Scotland, and wife Christina in Edinburgh. Both immigrated to the United States in their 20s. In 1916, William took a position with International Harvester. He worked in the accounting office, and by 1928, he became comptroller. William and Christina made their home in Highland Park. Their daughter Frances married Conrad Hilton. (Wisconsin Historical Society.)

Alexander Legge Jr. was born in 1866 in Wisconsin, as the son of Scottish immigrants. Alex Jr. worked as a ranch hand and later took a job with International Harvester. He eventually became president, serving from 1922 to 1929 during the "tractor wars" with Henry Ford. During World War I, he was served on the War Industries Board and the Federal Farm Board. Legge was an active Illinois St. Andrew Society member.

William Goldie was born in Kilmarnock, Scotland, and learned the building trade in Glasgow. He married Emma Somerville in 1852. William Goldie and Sons built portions of Fort Sheridan, Ferry Hall, and Old Main at Barat College in Lake Forest. After the Chicago fire, he built the first business block, including the Marshall Field building. Goldie was a member of the Illinois St. Andrew Society. (Library of Congress.)

William Mundie was born in Canada to Scottish parents. He trained as an architect and moved to Chicago in 1884. He became a partner with William LeBaron Jenney. Their firm were pioneers of the steel-framed skyscraper. Mundie was a member of the Illinois St. Andrew Society. In 1910, Mundie was the architect for the Scottish Old People's Home. William and Bessie Mundie made their home in Evanston.

William Mavor was born in Aberdeenshire, Scotland, in 1848. He came to Chicago at age 20 and started a contracting business. William married Mary Strang, a Scottish girl from the Scottish settlement of Milburn, Illinois, where he built a home for her family. William served four terms as a Chicago alderman and helped build bathhouses for the poor. (Historic Milburn Association.)

Mavor kept an office on Sheridan Road in Lake Forest. They built the J. Ogden Armour home in Lake Forest, which, today, is part of Lake Forest Academy and the home of Harold McCormick. Mavor built the Masonic temple, which, at that time, was the tallest building in Chicago. They built a portion of the Marshall Field Store and the Agriculture Building for the Chicago World's Fair. (HCLFLB.)

In 1835, John and Margaret (Clelland) Strang left Scotland with 8 of their 10 children. Three years later, the family settled on farmland in Millburn, Illinois. William Strang served on the board of the first bank in Lake Forest. Mary Strang (standing in center) married Scottish contractor William Mavor, who built a home for the Strang family on Grass Lake Road in Millburn. (Historic Millburn Association.)

Born in 1879, Morton Mavor was the oldest son of William and Mary Mavor. He earned an engineering degree from Purdue and joined the family business. He eventually became the company president. Morton made his home at 111 Laurel Avenue in Highland Park. He served on the board of the Highland Park National Bank. Mavor Lane in Highland Park is named for Morton. (Highland Park Historical Society.)

Three

MOVERS AND SHAKERS

In 1867, Philip Armour founded a slaughterhouse in Chicago. His family roots were in Scotland. Armour was an astute businessman and, within a decade, had turned a profit of over $1 million. Refrigerated rail cars soon meant that Armour meat could be shipped coast to coast. A biographical sketch reported, "Armour was one of the most generous supporters of the Scottish organization known as the Illinois St. Andrew Society."

Philip Danforth Armour III and cousin Lolita Armour are seen here in 1906. Philip Armour built an estate in Lake Bluff he called Tangley Oaks, where he employed Scottish-born gardeners Robert Dobbin and Robert Preston. Lolita was the only daughter of J. Ogden Armour. She was raised on the family estate Mellody Farm in west Lake Forest, which stretched over 1,000 acres.

J. Ogden Armour, the son of Philip, took control of Armour and Company. Annual sales boomed during World War I, and the company was valued at almost $1 billion; however, by 1922, Armour and Company was bankrupt due to declining meat prices and massive debts. But a seemingly worthless investment in a Texas oil refining business soon turned the family fortunes around.

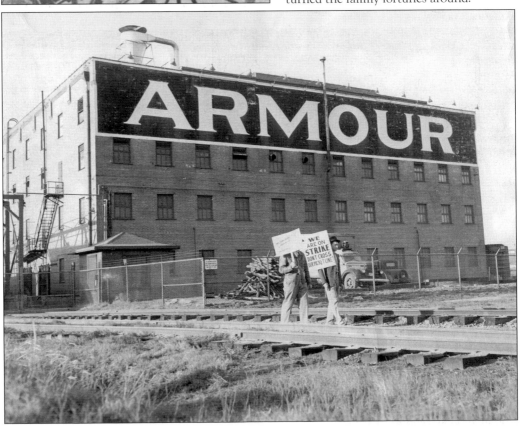

Joseph Badenoch came to Chicago from Scotland in the 1850s. In 1907, five men wagered to see who could walk from Milwaukee to Chicago in under 60 hours. Joseph joined in for fun. A race judge declared the task impossible because of a blinding snowstorm. But 53 hours later, 59-year-old Joseph Badenoch crossed the finish line. None of the other five completed the race. (The Badenoch family.)

In this photograph is Joseph Badenoch Jr. (left), Chicago Board of Trade president. The family summered in Lake Forest. Joseph Badenoch Sr. founded the Englewood Electric Company, and brother John Badenoch served Chicago as chief of police. Badenoch family members maintained a home in Lake Bluff until 1975.

William McCormick Blair Jr. is pictured here with wife Catherine in Denmark, where Blair served as US ambassador. William McCormick Blair Sr. was Scottish on both sides. His father, Edward, had married into the McCormick family. With financial backing from John and Douglas Stuart, two of the Scots who founded Quaker Oats, William founded his own investment firm, which is still in business today.

Edward McCormick Blair Jr. is seen here with Nancy Greene at a 1963 dinner hosted by Knight Cowles in Lake Forest. The Blair family had built a home in Lake Bluff on Lake Michigan after purchasing a portion of Crab Tree Farm. They later would buy most of the remaining property. Blair Park and Pool in Lake Bluff are named for the family.

The Buchanan family originated in Dumbarton, Scotland, and were members of the Illinois St. Andrew Society. In the late 1800s, they acquired the struggling Wilmington Star Coal Company. In 1898, Dewitt "Buck" Buchanan graduated from Purdue University and took over management of Wilmington Star. Buck changed the business name to Old Ben Coal Company. Soon, Old Ben grew into one of the nation's largest coal producers.

Dewitt Buchanan Jr. joined Old Ben in 1940 after graduating from Princeton. Dewitt made many safety improvements and pioneered the use of mining machines and conveyor belts. As president, he negotiated the sale of Old Ben to Standard Oil in 1968. DeWitt served as a director of Standard Oil until his retirement in 1988. Buchanan Hall at Lake Forest College is named for the family.

Harry Clow is seen third from the right. His family originated in Dumfriesshire, Scotland. The Clow home in Pennsylvania was a stop on the Underground Railroad. In Chicago, the family ran a successful cast-iron pipe business. Harry Clow married Elizabeth McNally, the daughter of Rand McNally. Harry would later become CEO of Rand McNally & Company. Harry and Elizabeth built an estate in Lake Bluff they named Landsdowne. (Library of Congress.)

William Stirling was born in Scotland and came to the United States in 1879. He served as an officer for Illinois Steel and made his home in Lake Forest. He was a frequent donor to the Illinois St. Andrew Society. In 1928, the Ridge Farm Preventorium was built by the family, and one of the buildings was named Stirling Hall. Today, it is the Grove Cultural Center. (HCLFLB.)

John "Jack" Crerar was born in Nova Scotia in 1857 to Scottish parents. Jack was sent to the prestigious King's School in Canterbury, England. After defending a classmate who was being punished by a teacher, Crerar was beaten for insubordination. Jack led a revolt. Students gathered provisions in their dorms and barricaded the doors, and several days of student rioting followed. Ringleader Crerar was promptly expelled. (King's School.)

After being expelled from the King's School, Jack Crerar (fourth row, second from left) attended Inverness Royal Academy in Scotland. Jack excelled as an athlete and as a student and seemed to prefer the less formal atmosphere in Scotland. Later, Jack attended Glasgow University. He remained in Glasgow after graduation and learned the shipping business working for Allan Gow and, later, Donaldson and Brothers Steamship Line. (Inverness Royal Academy.)

In 1879, Jack began work for fellow Scot William Stirling at Joliet Steel. At the time, several US steel companies were owned and operated by Scots. Crerar married Marie Owen, and the couple made their home in Chicago on Prairie Avenue, with their daughters Marie and Catherine. Jack Crerar would later partner with Floyd Clinch. The two men built their own successful coal business operating out of Chicago. (David Crerar.)

Jack Crerar bought 900 East Illinois Road in Lake Forest. He served as president of the Illinois St. Andrew Society and was a generous supporter of the Scottish Old People's Home. Crerar built the Dennison and Sherman Railway, which was the first interurban railway in Texas. Crerar's real estate holdings extended from Nova Scotia to Saskatchewan. Jack died in 1932 in the Illinois Road home. (HCLFLB.)

Robert Forgan (seated) and Robert Jr. (standing) in this c. 1880 photograph. The Forgan golf shop was located in St. Andrews, Scotland, along the 17th fairway of the Old Course. Robert's sons James Berwick Forgan and David Robertson Forgan were sent to Canada to take jobs as bank messengers. Both of the brothers later became bank presidents in Chicago. (Forgan Golf.)

In Canada in 1885, David Forgan married Agnes Kerr, whose father was born in Scotland. The couple had five children: Robert, Marion, Ethel, David Jr., and James. The Forgan family made their home at 1112 Greenwood in Evanston. David was an excellent golfer, and he won the very first Western Amateur Championship. (Library of Congress.)

James "Russ" Forgan, Fred Clark, and John Cudahy are seen here in June 1936, as young Crusaders opposed to Prohibition. James was the youngest son of David and Agnes Forgan. A 1922 Princeton graduate, Russ was friends with F. Scott Fitzgerald. James served as an intelligence officer for the Office of Strategic Services during World War II. After the war, he ran the investment firm of Forgan, Field and Glore.

Ginevra Pirie (in white) and Ada Forgan are pictured around 1954 at Shoreacres in Lake Bluff. A teenaged Ginevra had been a pen pal of F. Scott Fitzgerald and was his muse for Daisy Buchanan in *The Great Gatsby*. Ada married Russ Forgan, who was a Princeton classmate of Fitzgerald's. Russ and Ada made their home in Lake Forest for a while before moving to New York.

James Berick Forgan Jr. (left) was born in Minnesota in 1890. Like his father, he also became a banker and eventually rose to president. In 1914, he married Margaret Meeker, and the couple built a large stone house on Ahwanee Lane in Lake Forest, overlooking the Onwentsia Club golf course. In 1964, James Jr. was honored by the Illinois St. Andrew Society as its "Distinguished Citizen."

James Forgan Jr. (left) and Marshall Field III are seen here in 1941. James Forgan Sr. served as president of the Illinois St. Andrew Society. In 1917, he decided that for the first time in more than 70 years, ladies should be invited to attend the Scottish Anniversary Charity Dinner. A strict Presbyterian, he urged the men "to reduce their drinking and story-telling, so that the ladies would feel comfortable."

The Keiths ran a wholesale clothing business in Chicago. The family originated in Keith, Scotland. Stanley Keith married Dorothy Leslie, whose family was from Brechin, Scotland, and the couple lived in Lake Forest with their two daughters. Tragically, Dorothy Keith was killed in a car accident when she and Stanley were hit head-on by a speeding driver. Stanley Keith was badly injured but survived the accident.

Later, Stanley Keith married the widow Helen Shedd (right). The Shedd Aquarium was named for her family. Stanley and Helen lived on Lake Road in Lake Forest. Daughter Leslie Keith married Robert Stuart MacDonald, and the newlyweds also made their home in Lake Forest. Robert's mother was Margaret Stuart, whose father helped found Quaker Oats. Robert Stuart MacDonald also worked for Quaker Oats.

Robert Stuart MacDonald Jr. was born in 1936, the son of Leslie Keith and Robert MacDonald Sr. At Saint Mary's Church in Lake Forest, he married Leola Armour of Lake Bluff. The Armour family also originated in Scotland. In 1974, Robert attended the Illinois St. Andrew Society Anniversary dinner, where his uncle Angus MacDonald was honored with the Distinguished Citizen Award.

Scots-born J.J. Murdock lived in Lake Bluff. He engineered a merger of Joseph Kennedy's movie business and the Keith Theaters. The company made movies such as King Kong and signed Katharine Hepburn, John Barrymore, and Fred Astaire. The movie business came to be known as RKO Pictures. The "K" in RKO is for Keith. John Murdock's amassed a fortune of more than $60 million and donated much of it for cancer research. (The Murdock family.)

Robert Patterson Lamont was born in 1867 in Detroit. All of his grandparents were born in Scotland. Lamont worked as an engineer at the Columbian Exposition in Chicago. He lived in Lake Forest with his wife, Helen, and children Dorothy, Gertrude, and Robert Jr. In 1929, Lamont was appointed the secretary of commerce under President Hoover. Hoover attended the wedding of Robert's daughter Gertrude. (Library of Congress.)

James Kirk was born in Glasgow, Scotland, where his family ran a successful soap business. Wanting to set out on his own, he relocated to Utica, New York, in 1818, where he founded Kirk Soaps. In 1859, he moved to Chicago, where he built a factory along the Chicago River, where Fort Dearborn had once been. The original factory was lost in the Great Chicago Fire. Eventually, a five-story brick building was erected on North Water Street to replace the lost structure. By 1900, the Kirk Soap factory was producing 100 million pounds of soap per year, and the company branched out into perfumes and other toiletries. (Kirk Soaps.)

Several family members entered the Kirk Soap business, including Milton William Kirk, who was the son of the founder James Kirk. Milton grew up in Evanston, Illinois. Milton's older son Milton Beckwith Kirk died at age 40 in France, where he served as the American consul. His daughter Emma lived in Winnetka with her husband, John McEwen, whose father was from Scotland.

After Harvard, grandson Walter Kirk joined Kirk Soaps and moved to Lake Forest. In a bankruptcy case, daughter Beatrice listed her father as the largest creditor and valued her possessions at $98 of clothes. Walter was asked whether Beatrice might have more possessions. He testified, "If she has as many clothes as she has listed then she has too many."

Alexander Kirkland was president of the Illinois St. Andrew Society from 1879 to 1881. Born in Scotland in 1834, he was a Glasgow University graduate. In Chicago, he was building commissioner and architect of the new city hall constructed in 1881. Weymouth Kirkland (pictured) was the grandson of Alexander. Weymouth graduated from the Kent College of Law and was a member of the Illinois St. Andrew Society. (Kirkland & Ellis Archives.)

In 1909, Robert "the Colonel" McCormick founded a law firm. His grandfather Joseph Medill was the publisher of the *Chicago Tribune*. The Medill family was Ulster Scots. Weymouth Kirkland joined the firm in 1915. The firm was later renamed for the four managing Scottish partners—McCormick, Kirkland, Patterson & Fleming. The Medill, McCormick, and Patterson families were related through marriage. Joseph Medill McCormick is pictured here.

In a landmark case, Kirkland defended the *Tribune* after an editorial called Henry Ford, an anarchist, and Ford sued for libel. After a three-month trial, the jury awarded Ford 6¢ for damages and 6¢ for costs. The *Tribune* refused to pay, and Ford collected nothing. Kirkland went on to win other freedom-of-the-press cases for other newspapers and the Associated Press.

Weymouth Kirkland is seated on the far left, with George Halas standing behind him. Standing in the top right is Philip R. Clarke Sr., who cofounded the investment firm Chicago Corporation. Clarke's family were from Scotland and lived in Ulster for one generation before they immigrated to the United States.

Robert Archibald Fleming was from Kilwinning, Scotland, and he brought his young family to the Braidwood, Illinois, area, where he worked as a coal miner. After a mine collapse, Robert was made an inspector. The family moved to Chicago, where Robert worked as a court clerk. His wife, Jane, became one of the first female school principals in Chicago. Joseph Fleming (pictured) did not follow his father into the coal mines. Joseph graduated from law school and worked as an assistant state's attorney. Later, he joined the firm of Kirkland and Ellis, where he became a partner. Joseph and wife, Lily, had five children and bought Woodleigh on Sheridan Road in Lake Forest. Joseph was the chair of the Lake Forest College Board of Trustees. (Courtesy of the Fleming family.)

Cyrus McCormick founded a company to manufacture harvesting machines, which is known as International Harvester today. The McCormick family were Ulster Scots. The McCormick reaper sold well, and operations were moved to Chicago. Within a generation, the family went from farmers to manufacturers on an enormous scale, operating out of several Midwestern manufacturing plants.

Harold Fowler McCormick Jr. is seen here with Harvester employees. His parents, Harold Sr. and Edith (Rockefeller) McCormick, built an estate they called Villa Turicum, which covered 300 acres in far southeast Lake Forest. Walden was built for Cyrus McCormick II on 80 lakefront acres just to the north. Cyrus McCormick III lived nearby in a house called Argyllshire, named after a region of Scotland.

John T. McCutcheon (second from left) was born in Indiana to Scottish parents. He graduated from Purdue in 1889. McCutcheon Hall and the Highlander Club at Purdue are both named for the family. John became a cartoonist for the *Chicago Tribune* and won the Pulitzer Prize in 1932.

In 1917, McCutcheon married Evelyn Shaw, the daughter of architect Howard Van Doren Shaw. A line of the Shaw family descended from Ulster Scots. Shaw's first job was working for Scottish-born architect William Mundie. Some report that McCutcheon hosted Scottish-themed parties held behind the family home on Green Bay Road, complete with bagpipers. (Library of Congress.)

The Mackey Memorial Building at the Lake Bluff Children's home was a gift of Harry and Callae McIntosh. Harry was born in Aberdeenshire. In Chicago, he entered the real estate and investment business. The family owned a home on Sheridan Road in Lake Forest. Callae was Scottish, too; her maiden name was Mackey, and she was a MacKay on her maternal side. (Photograph by Kraig Moreland.)

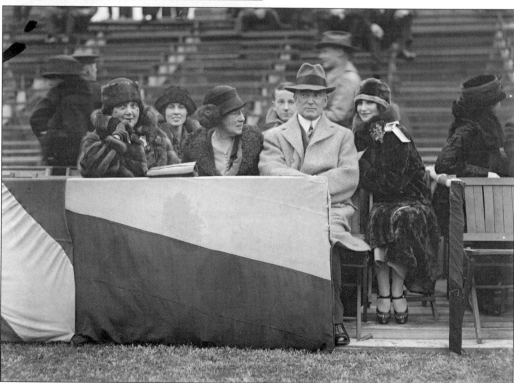

William Moffett, wife Jeannette (far left), and five children, including Janet (far right), lived in Lake Forest. Each day, as William drove north from Lake Forest to Great Lakes, he crossed a bridge in Lake Bluff over a ravine. He dispatched a crew of naval engineers to repair the bridge in Lake Bluff, and the road was renamed Moffett Road in his honor. (Library of Congress.)

The Moffett family came from Argyllshire. William Moffett was born in South Carolina in 1869 and graduated from the US Naval Academy in 1890. He was awarded the Medal of Honor for his actions during the battle of Veracruz. During World War I, William was the commander of the Great Lakes Naval Training Center. (Library of Congress.)

William Moffett established a naval aviator training program and introduced the use of aircraft carriers. He came to be known as the "Air Admiral." In 1933, the USS *Akron*, with Admiral Moffett aboard, flew a mission along the coast of New England. The ship was caught in a violent windstorm and crashed into the Atlantic Ocean. A total of 73 of the 76 onboard died, including Admiral Moffett. (Library of Congress.)

George Alexander "Mac" McKinlock Jr. was Scottish on both sides; his mother was a Wallace, and his grandmother was a Neil. His father was a financier and active golfer. The family owned an estate in Lake Forest called Brown Gables. Young Mac was a fine horseman. He attended Harvard, where he played football and joined the ROTC. (Library of Congress.)

The Alexander McKinlock Memorial Campus, Northwestern University. Mac McKinlock Jr. was with a machine gun group in France and is believed to be the first Lake Forester killed in World War I. The Lake Forest American Legion Post is named in his honor as are buildings at both Harvard and Northwestern.

William McLennan and Julia MacLeod came from a tiny Scottish fishing village called Stornoway. The young couple moved to Duluth, Minnesota, where, in 1873, son Donald Roderick McLennan was born. In 1905, Donald cofounded his own insurance brokerage firm, Marsh and McLennan, a multi-billion dollar business that survives to this day. Donald named his Lake Forest home Stornoway, where he and wife, Katherine, raised six children. Son George was a pilot who lost his life serving his country in World War II. Donald served on the boards of both the Armour Company and the First National Bank of Lake Forest—two companies deep Scottish connections. Dame Flora MacLeod, the chief of Clan MacLeod, visited the family home.

The Mitchell family originated in Edinburgh and were successful bankers in Chicago. John Mitchell Jr. attended Yale University and served as a Navy aviator during World War I. In 1921, he married Lolita Armour. In 1925, he helped found National Air Transport, which later merged with three other competitors and became United Airlines. John served on the board of directors and continued as a company director until 1970.

During World War I, William Mitchell was a Navy pilot. In 1918, he married Ginevra King, the inspiration for Daisy Buchanan in *The Great Gatsby*. The couple later divorced, and William married Anne Wood (pictured). William founded the investment firm Mitchell, Hutchins & Co., where he served as chairman until his retirement in 1964. At his Lake Forest estate, he employed a Scottish-born chauffeur and gardener.

Scottish-born James Norris founded a shipping and grain business in Canada. His grandson James E. Norris was born in 1879 in Montreal and joined the family business at age 18. By age 28, James was Norris and Company president. The company headquarters were moved to Chicago. James bought an estate in Lake Forest, where he raised son Bruce and daughter Marguerite. Norris employed Scottish-born Thomas Dobbin, who lived on the estate and worked as a caretaker. (National Hockey League.)

The Norris family were financial backers of the Chicago Stadium and eventually became the owners of the Detroit Red Wings. In 1944, the Norris family also became the majority owner of the Chicago Black Hawks. After graduating from Yale, son Bruce Norris (pictured), joined the family business. He served in the Navy during World War II and eventually was the sole owner of the Red Wings. (National Hockey League.)

Marguerite Ann Norris was born in 1927 (pictured with her father, James). When James Norris died in 1952, Marguerite became president of the Detroit Red Wings. She was the first female chief executive of a National Hockey League team. During the three years she served as president, the Red Wings won the Stanley Cup twice, and her name is engraved on the trophy.

After the Red Wings won the Stanley Cup in 1955, Marguerite resigned her position as president, and her brother Bruce took over operations. Bruce was part of three Stanley Cup Championships and was elected chairman of the National Hockey League Board of Governors. Bruce and his father, James, were both inducted into the National Hockey League Hall of Fame. The Norris Trophy is named for the family.

(CX1) CHICAGO, Dec. 14--ADDS FEMININE TOUCH TO HOCKEY--Marguerite Ann Norris, who yesterday became president of the Detroit Red Wings hockey team and Olympia Stadium in Detroit, relaxes as she scans through a hockey program in her home in suburban Lake Forest today. Miss Norris,

The Dobbin family was from Broughty Ferry, Scotland. Brothers Robert and Thomas both secured work in Lake Forest. Robert worked and lived at Tangley Oaks, the estate of Philip Armour. Thomas worked for the Norris family, who hosted the wedding of his daughter on the family estate. (The Dobbin family.)

Anna Maria Emily Bernie was born in Glasgow in 1881. In 1907, she married Harold Smith in London. Harold was the son of Byron Smith of Chicago and Lake Forest, whose family helped found Northern Trust. The newlyweds arrived in the US in 1908, had four children, and split their time between Chicago and Lake Forest.

Elizabeth Smith is seen here in 1935 playing tennis in the Bahamas. She was the oldest daughter of Anna and Harold Smith. Elizabeth married Gardner Brown, whose father, William Brown, was born in Edinburgh, Scotland. The Smith and Brown families were members of the Illinois St. Andrew Society.

Gardner Brown graduated from Yale and was a lieutenant commander in World War II. He served as president of the Chicago Better Government Association and was a Lake Forest College trustee. By 1947, the couple had bought their own home in Lake Forest just off of Sheridan Road, which was later donated to Lake Forest College. Today, Brown House serves as the home of the college president. (HCLFLB.)

Austin Niblack was born in 1885. His family had come to the United States from Clackmannan, Scotland. In 1915, Austin married Helen Cudahy of the famous meatpacking family. The couple made their home on Old Mill Road in Lake Forest, and Austin worked as an investment broker. For many years, he was master of the hounds at Onwentsia Club and the Mill Creek Hunt Club. Austin is pictured here with his children Albert and Helen.

Thomas Murdoch (pictured) was born and raised in Forres, Scotland. Simon Summerville Reid was from Duffus, just a few miles away. In Chicago, Reid and Murdoch operated a wholesale grocery business under the name Monarch Foods. As Chicago and the Midwest grew, business boomed, and the Reid Murdoch Building was erected along the Chicago River. (The Murdock family.)

Simon Summerville Reid was described by an early Lake Forest resident as "tall and slight, with a pronounced Scottish accent, dignified, with old fashioned courtly manners." In 1915, the Reid Murdoch building on the Chicago River became a makeshift hospital and morgue after the SS *Eastland* capsized. (Lake Forest College.)

Thomas Murdoch never married. His will directed $2 million to various charities, including a generous gift to the Scottish Old People's home. Old friends Reid and Murdoch ended their lives as they began them—very near one another. Both are buried in Lake Forest Cemetery, just a few paces apart. Fittingly, today, the Reid Murdoch building houses another Scottish business. (Encyclopedia Britannica.)

In Lake Forest, Simon Reid built a home he called "the Lilacs" across from the entrance to Lake Forest College, where he lived with his family. He built Reid Hall for Lake Forest Academy and Reid Hall for Lake Forest College. He later built Glen Rowan House, where his daughter lived. (Lake Forest College.)

Hugh "Robbie" Robertson was born in Glasgow in 1887. He built crystal radio receivers as a hobby. He came to Chicago, where he worked for an auto dealership before joining the fledgling radio manufacturer Zenith Corporation. Robbie and his wife, Mabel, owned a home on the west side of Lake Forest. The family later built a home on Negaunee Lane overlooking Onwentsia golf course. (Zenith Corporation.)

Hugh "Robbie" Robertson is pictured at his 45th Zenith anniversary party. Robbie appeared on the cover of *Forbes* magazine in 1961. Robertson served as a Zenith director for more than 40 years. In 1958, he was made president, CEO, and then board chairman until his retirement in 1964. Robertson was an active member of the Illinois St. Andrew Society.

Robert Stevenson and his wife, Marianne Scott Dill, were married in Northern Ireland and came to the United States in 1860. They were both Ulster Scots. No fewer than 12 family members served as Church of Scotland Presbyterian ministers. In Chicago, the couple had six children, and Robert Stevenson worked as a wholesale druggist. (Ed Stevenson.)

Robert Stevenson Jr. and sister Sarah are seen here around 1888. Robert became an investment broker, and his younger brother Richard served in a Field Artillery Division during World War I, where he met and married volunteer nurse, Helen Farwell of Lake Forest. Helen and Richard would eventually make their home in Lake Forest. Richard started his career working in the family business but eventually became a bond broker. (Ed Stevenson.)

Seated in the bottom left is John Archibald "Archie" Stevenson at a Scottish-themed party held at the Lake Forest Winter Club around 1951. Other Scots in the photograph include Stanton and Jean Armour and Pete Clow. Even multiple generations removed from their Scottish-born ancestors, their national identity remained strong. (Ed Stevenson.)

Adlai Stevenson Jr. (center) is seen here with sons Adlai III (left) and John (right) in 1952. Adlai Ewing Stevenson Jr. was born in 1900. Both the Stevenson and Ewing families had come to the United States from Scotland. In 1935, Stevenson purchased land in Mettawa, Illinois, where he built his home. Adlai served as governor of Illinois from 1949 to 1953 and was the Democratic Party's nomination for president in 1952 and 1956.

William Templeton was a sugar merchant in Glasgow who came to Chicago in 1864. William became a member of the Chicago Board of Trade, where his son James Stuart Templeton joined him in business. The history of the board of trade reports that Templeton made $300,000 in his first 14 months in Chicago. Pictured in the top right is Kenneth Stuart Templeton. (University of Wisconsin.)

After graduating from the University of Wisconsin in 1911, Kenneth Stuart Templeton (left) joined the family business. Kenneth made his home at 1250 Elm Tree Road in Lake Forest. Younger brother Stuart John Templeton was a lawyer and built his house Windswept at 1300 North Green Bay Road in Lake Forest. The family donated generously to the Illinois St. Andrew Society.

Thomas Wilson was born in Canada in 1868 to a Scottish family. Thomas started work in the stockyards checking railroad cars but rose quickly through the ranks. By 1916, he was running his own company with operations stretching from Canada to Brazil. Thomas hired Murdo MacKenzie from Tain, Scotland, to be his manager overseeing herds of cattle distributed over nine million acres.

By 1918, Wilson and Company meatpacking assets were valued at over $129 million, which is over a billion dollars today. Thomas moved to Lake Forest and helped found Knollwood Golf Club on land just north of his estate. Thomas established Edellyn Farm on 450 acres just north of Lake Forest, named for his son Ed and daughter Helen. Thomas raised Scottish Clydesdale horses and champion Scottish shorthorn cattle.

Son Edward Wilson followed his father into the business. Like fellow Scots, the Wilsons were thrifty and viewed unused animal parts as waste. They used animal by-products, which were usually discarded, to instead create tennis racket strings. The company soon branched out into golf balls, sports jerseys, and golf bags. It is this little side business for which Thomas is remembered today: the Wilson Sporting Goods Company.

Three generations of the Wilson clan at Wrigley Field to watch the Chicago Cubs. From left to right are Thomas Edward Wilson, grandson Edward Thomas Wilson, and Edward Foss Wilson. At one point, Wilson and Company supplied uniforms for both the Chicago Cubs and Chicago White Sox.

Arthur Young was born in Glasgow, Scotland. His degree was in law, but he became interested in banking. In 1890, he moved to the United States and formed Arthur Young & Company. Young was an innovator and positioned himself as a business advisor as much as an accountant. He was a member of the Illinois St. Andrew Society and served as the auditor. (Ernst and Young.)

In 1924, Arthur Young allied with the prominent British firm Broads Paterson & Co and opened offices around the world. Arthur owned a home in Lake Forest on Green Bay Road and another in South Carolina. In 1989, Arthur Young and Company merged with AC Ernst to form Ernst and Young, which today employs more than 230,000 worldwide. (Ernst and Young.)

Four

QUAKER OATS

George Douglas was born in Caithness, Scotland. He and his five brothers moved to Canada, where George married Margaret Boyd, who was born to Ulster Scots parents. In Illinois, George worked for the Northwestern Railroad. In Iowa, George met John Stuart from Banffshire, Scotland, and they formed Douglas and Stuart Oats, which would eventually operate under the name Quaker Oats. (John Douglas.)

Pictured from left to right are George Jr., Walter, and Edward Douglas, the children of George and Martha Douglas. After attending Shattuck Military Academy in Minnesota, the boys would join the family business. George Jr. and brother Walter formed the Douglas Starch Company and, later, Midland Linseed Oil, out of Minneapolis. Walter died in the *Titanic* after giving up his place in a lifeboat to his maid. (John Douglas.)

James Douglas Sr. was born in Canada. He joined Douglas and Stuart Oats, eventually serving as president. James and his wife, Inez, bought a home in Lake Forest, where they raised sons James Jr. and Donald. The boys were classmates of F. Scott Fitzgerald at Princeton. Fitzgerald autographed a book for the Douglas family, thanking them for hosting him for a summer month. (John Douglas.)

After graduating from Princeton in 1914, Donald Douglas served in the US Army. Later, he joined the family business—Quaker Oats. In 1919, he married Lake Forester Martha Clow, and the couple lived on Green Bay Road, next door to Donald's parents. Donald continued to work for Quaker Oats until he retired in 1957, just before his 65th birthday. Donald Douglas is pictured here with Anne (Wood) Mitchell, who had married Scottish-American William Mitchell. At one point, nine of the twelve workers living on the two Douglas properties on Green Bay Road in Lake Forest were born in Scotland. Donald and his employees hosted Scottish-themed bonfire parties attended by neighbors and their employees. It is said that these parties were the inspiration for the annual Bagpipes and Bonfires fundraisers held each fall in Lake Forest today.

Joseph Betts McCall from Ayr, Scotland, had served in the Cameron Highlanders. He was a sheet metal worker and lived with his family in Lake Forest. When the various Scottish families would gather for parties at the home of Donald Douglas on Green Bay Road, Joseph was the piper. To this day, Bagpipes and Bonfires is an annual fundraiser in Lake Forest. (The McCall family.)

James Douglas Jr. graduated from Princeton in 1920. In 1928, he married fellow Lake Forester Grace Farwell McGann (pictured). The couple eventually bought a home at 1 Stone Gate Road, where they raised their four boys. Sadly, Grace died of cancer at age 42. (John Douglas.)

At first, James Jr. worked as an attorney in Chicago, but in 1932 he became the assistant secretary of the treasury. He returned to Chicago to practice law with Gardner, Carton and Douglas. In 1953, he began work for the Eisenhower administration. He served as secretary of the US Air Force and helped establish the Air Force Academy, where Douglas Field is named in his honor. (John Douglas.)

Air Force secretary James H. Douglas Jr. is on the right in a 1957 photograph holding a model of a jet engine. At one point, Douglas worked for the investment firm of Forgan, Field and Glore. The Forgan family was from St. Andrews, Scotland. In 1961, President Eisenhower presented Douglas with the Medal of Freedom.

The Douglas family were generous supporters of the Illinois St. Andrew Society and never forgot their roots. For many years, they donated truckloads of food and clothes to be distributed to needy Scots in Chicago. They also supported the Scottish Old People's Home in North Riverside. James H. Douglas Jr. died in 1988.

John Stuart was born in Banffshire, Scotland. The Stuart family moved to Canada and started a grain business. In 1893, John moved his family to Cedar Rapids, Iowa, where he met George Douglas, who was from Caithness, Scotland. Together, the two Scots founded their own grain milling business, a company that would later operate under the name Quaker Oats.

John Stuart's son Robert Stuart was born in Ontario, Canada, in 1852. The family moved to Iowa, where Robert joined the family grain business. Robert married Margaret Sharrar, who also had Scottish lineage. The family and their grain business eventually moved to Chicago. Robert and Margaret raised three children: John, Margaret, and Robert. The family owned a home on fashionable South Woodlawn Avenue.

Robert Douglas Stuart Sr. was born in 1886 in Illinois. He was the next generation of the family to join the grain business. Robert married Harriet Dixon McClure; both the Dixon and McClure families were Ulster Scots. The couple lived at 528 Mayflower Road in Lake Forest, and Robert would eventually serve as president of Quaker Oats.

Pres. Dwight Eisenhower (left) is seen walking with Robert Douglas Stuart. R. Douglas Stuart was a delegate to the 1952 Republican National Convention. In 1953, President Eisenhower named Stuart as the US ambassador to Canada. R. Douglas Stuart also served on the board of the Illinois St. Andrew Society.

R. Douglas Stuart Jr. entered the business after his father. He served as CEO of Quaker Oats from 1966 to 1981. He also served as the US ambassador to Norway from 1984 to 1989. Stuart family members owned homes in Lake Forest on Elm Tree and Mayflower Road, where Scots-born Margaret McRobbie and Mary Dunlop lived and worked for the family. (HCLFLB.)

Five

CARSON, PIRIE, AND SCOTT

John Pirie was born in Errol, Scotland, in 1827, where he was raised and educated. John served an apprenticeship in Glasgow, learning the dry goods business and later worked for his uncle Henry Hawkins. Brothers George and Robert Scott also worked for Hawkins, as did Samuel Carson. John married Sarah Carson, the sister of his friend and business partner Samuel Carson.

Determined to start a business of their own, John Pirie and Samuel Carson (pictured) set sail for the United States in 1854. They first found work in New York, but eventually, they ventured west and opened a store in LaSalle, Illinois. The Carson & Pirie business flourished, and the young partners opened more stores, eventually deciding to relocate to booming Chicago in 1864.

Robert Scott worked for Henry Hawkins in Northern Ireland, learning the dry goods business. The Scott family were originally from Dalkeith, Scotland, and had moved to Northern Ireland. The Scott brothers relocated to Central Illinois and went into business for themselves. In Chicago, the brothers partnered with their old friends, thus the creation of Carson, Pirie and Scott. Scott family members made their home in Winnetka.

In 1867, Scottish-born Andrew MacLeish was hired to run the Chicago retail stores. He organized an effort that saved much of the merchandise from the Great Chicago Fire in 1871. The firm quickly rebuilt and expanded. Over the next 40 years, the population of Chicago grew by more than one million, and business boomed. Andrew built an estate in Glencoe, which he called "Craigie Lea."

Andrew's son Archibald became the librarian of Congress and created the position of US poet laureate. He wrote, "My father came from a very old country in the north and far away, and he belonged to an old strange race, the race older than any other. He did not talk of his country but he sang bits of old songs with words that he said no one could understand anymore."

John and Sarah Pirie had three boys and three girls. Son John T. Pirie (pictured) married Sophie Hunter, whose parents were also Scottish. The couple moved to Lake Forest and made their home at 930 Rosemary Road, with a gardener's cottage on Mayflower Road and a home for staff on Maple Court. John T. Pirie worked in the family business and served as Lake Forest mayor from 1911 to 1914.

In Lake Forest, John and Sarah Pirie employed several Scots, including William and Lillian Mackie, Rachael McLure, and Annie McInnis. They hired coachman William Heaney. The Heaney family were Ulster Scots, and William's mother was born in Scotland. William and Sophie Pirie are shown here seated in the Heaney home in Lake Forest, celebrating William's 93rd birthday. (The Heaney family.)

John Taylor Pirie Jr. also entered the family business and eventually became president of Carson, Pirie and Scott. Pictured here in 1954, from left to right are Bruce McLeish, chairman of the board; Frederick H. Scott, chairman of the finance committee; and John T. Pirie Jr., president. The founding families of Carson, Pirie and Scott were still firmly in control of the business.

John. T. Pirie Jr. (right) divorced his first wife and later married the former Ginevra (King) Mitchell (far left). Ginevra and her first husband William Mitchell lived on Rosemary Road in Lake Forest, across the street from the Pirie home. Teenaged Ginevra and F. Scott Fitzgerald had exchanged letters for years, and Ginevra served as the muse for Daisy Buchanan in *The Great Gatsby*.

John Scott was born in 1870. He spent one year at Brown University before he joined the family business. In 1901, he became a partner in Carson, Pirie and Scott. In 1899, John married Emily Cluett. The couple lived in Winnetka, where they raised daughters Elizabeth and Barbara. The Scott family were members of the Onwentsia Club in Lake Forest. (James Welles.)

Elizabeth Scott married Edward Welles. Her sister Barbara Scott married Donald Welles, twin brother of Edward. (Pictured is Donald's son James Welles.) The two couples lived next to one another on Ahwahnee Road in Lake Forest. During World War II, Edward Welles did not serve because he was in a war-critical industry. Edward later served at Lake Forest mayor. During World War II, Donald served as a head procurement officer in Washington. (James Welles.)

Six

MARSHALL FIELD AND COMPANY

In 1856, Marshall Field arrived in boomtown Chicago and took a job working for a wholesale business at a salary of $400 per year. Field himself could claim almost no Scottish ancestry; however, he married Nannie Douglas Scott, a girl of Scottish heritage. Field seemed to have an affinity for Scots and hired many. In early photographs, his son and grandson are seen wearing kilts.

James Simpson was born in Glasgow in 1874. At age 17, he landed a job at Marshall Field and Company. Within a year, he was working as a personal clerk for Field and asked for a raise. Marshall Field replied, "Young man, at your age I was making $3 a week!" "Well, Mr. Field," replied Simpson, "perhaps that is all you were worth." Field gave Jimmy the raise.

James Simpson married Jessie McLaren, and the couple made their home in Glencoe. Jessie's father was born in Scotland. After Marshall Field died, James and fellow Scot John McKinlay bought up shares of Marshall Field and Company, and by 1923, James was president. Simpson went on to oversee the building of the Merchandise Mart, ran the Chicago Plan Commission, and later helped save Commonwealth Edison from near bankruptcy.

James Simpson is pictured in 1931 with son James Simpson Jr., who was a candidate for congress. In Lake Forest, the first Field's retail store outside of Chicago opened. Simpson was an Onwentsia member; his sister lived in Lake Forest, and his son John McLaren Simpson lived on Shoreacres Road. John and his wife later lived in an almost identical house they built on Lake Road.

John Simpson (left), the son of James and Jessie Simpson, is seen here in 1932 with friend Watson Armour in New York City, ready to board the SS *Aquitania* for a seven-month hunt in India and Africa. James also helped fund a Field Museum collection expedition to Asia led by the Roosevelt brothers. A room at the Field Museum is named for Simpson.

James Simpson Jr. is seen on his honeymoon in Bermuda after marrying the former Ella Snelling in 1931. James Jr. would later make his home on Storybrook Farm in Wadsworth, Illinois. He was a Harvard graduate and served in the 73rd US Congress from 1933 to 1935.

In 1939, James Simpson Jr. was admitted to the Illinois bar. He joined the US Marine Corps in 1943 and served for three years, including two years in the Pacific. Simpson served as a director of Marshall Field and Company from 1931 to 1960. Later, Captain Simpson served as an aid to Robert Stevens, the secretary of the Army.

After James Simpson, Scottish-born John McKinlay ran Marshall Field's until 1935, when James "Mac" McKinsey was hired. Mac, born in St. Louis to a Scottish family, was the founder of McKinsey & Company, which is still in business. He made his home at 1570 Waukegan Road in Lake Forest. McKinsey died suddenly in late 1937. (McKinsey and Company.)

By 1943, Marshall Field and Company again had a Scot serving as president. Hughston McBain (far right) was born in 1902 and began his career with Marshall Field and Company as a bill adjuster. He then took a job as an errand boy for company chairman John Shedd. A week before turning 41, he was elected youngest president in company history.

Hughston McBain and his wife, Margaret, made their home at 466 Poplar Avenue in Winnetka, where they raised son James and daughters Margaret and Grace. They employed Scottish-born Mary Bisset. The McBains are seen at the wedding of their daughter Margaret to David Hagues.

Hughston McBain served as the first president of the Chicago Curling Club. He retired from Marshall Field's in 1958 after serving as chief executive officer for 15 years but remained a board member until 1973. McBain was also the 21st chief of Clan McBain. He was an active member of the Illinois St. Andrew Society and, in 1967, was the recipient of the Distinguished Citizen Award.

Seven

Distinguished Citizens

James McMillan was born in 1881 in Broughty Ferry, Scotland. In the United States, he took a position with the Wander Company, makers of Ovaltine. He began his 50-year career as a clerk and later served 27 years as company president. McMillan owned a lakefront estate at 445 Sheridan Road in Winnetka. He was an active member of the Illinois St. Andrew Society and the 1964 Distinguished Citizen.

Pictured here are Hughston McBain (left) and R. Douglas Stuart (right). Stuart was a 1964 Illinois St. Andrew Society Distinguished Citizen. The Stuart family have long been supporters of the Illinois St. Andrew Society. In the early 1900s, the family donated 1,400 pounds of poultry feed to the Scottish Old People's Home to aid their chicken and egg operation. It was recorded that 116 dozen eggs had been collected in one month alone.

Dr. James Campbell, president of Rush St. Luke's Medical Center, is seen here in 1976. Dr. Campbell was the Illinois St. Andrew Society Distinguished Citizen in 1975. Campbell joined the hospital's cardiology department in 1948. He performed the first heart catheterization in Chicago. He served as the College of Nursing's first president. Under his guidance, the institution expanded from two to four colleges. Dr. Campbell made his home in Lake Forest.

In 1965, Chief Judge William Campbell was named Illinois St. Andrew Society Distinguished Citizen. Campbell was born in Chicago, and his father John was born in Glasgow. Campbell received his law degree from Loyola University Chicago School of Law. As a federal prosecutor, he helped convict Al Capone of tax evasion. Judge Campbell lived in Highland Park with his wife and daughter.

Pictured in 1950, from left to right, are Harold Ickes, Edward Sparling, Leo Lerner, and Judge William Campbell are seen here in 1950. In 1965, Campbell granted mobster Sam Giancana immunity and ordered him to testify. Giancana refused and spent the next year in jail. Campbell was passed over by President Johnson for a Supreme Court position. Years later, Campbell said, "Although I knew Johnson intimately and personally, he was bigoted enough not to want two Catholics on the Supreme Court."

Pictured here are Marguerite Church and Dr. J. Roscoe Miller. Dr. Miller was the 12th president of Northwestern University, serving between 1949 and 1970. The James Roscoe Miller Campus was constructed on lake fill and extended the eastern edge of the campus 1,000 feet into Lake Michigan. The project would increase the university's educational land holdings from 85 to 159 acres. Dr. Miller was the 1966 Illinois St. Andrew Society Distinguished Citizen.

Lawrence Kimpton and his wife, Mary, are pictured in 1957. Kimpton served as president of the University of Chicago from 1950 until 1960. At the 1969 Illinois St. Andrew Society anniversary dinner, Kimpton received the Distinguished Citizen Award. Kimpton had first come to the University of Chicago to serve as chief administrator of the laboratory engaged in the construction of the atomic bomb.

Fairfax Cone's father was a mining engineer. His mother, Isabelle, was a teacher. Fairfax earned an English degree and took a job as an advertising clerk with the *San Francisco Examiner*. Cone later joined the Lord and Thomas advertising agency, where he caught the attention of CEO Albert Lasker. Lasker wished to retire, and in 1942, his firm became Foote, Cone and Belding.

Fairfax Cone was honored as the Illinois St. Andrew Society Distinguished Citizen in 1968, along with Gov. Richard Ogilvie. Fairfax and his wife (center) are seen here with Millicent Stewart (far left) and Russell Stewart (far right). Fairfax Cone is often called "the father of modern advertising."

In 1970, Foster Glendale McGaw was the Illinois St. Andrew Society Distinguished Citizen. His father was a Presbyterian missionary. His maternal grandfather was also born in Scotland. After serving in the US Marine Corps, McGaw founded American Hospital Supply Corporation in 1922. The company eventually sold product to 95 percent of all American hospitals. In 1985, American Hospital Supply was purchased by Baxter Laboratories for $3.8 billion.

This image was captured during the 1972 ground breaking at the National College of Education. McGaw said the biggest factor that contributed to his company's success was an "effort to give more than we get." McGaw funded many buildings, including McGaw Memorial Hall and McGaw Medical Center at Northwestern University and the McGaw YMCA in Evanston. McGaw died in Lake Forest in 1986.

Arthur MacDougall Wood (left) was the 1971 Illinois St. Andrew Society Distinguished Citizen. He was born and raised in Highland Park. He graduated from Princeton and then Harvard Law. In 1941, he joined the Army Air Corps as a lieutenant colonel and helped plan the strategic bombing of Germany. Gen. Robert Wood, Sears chairman, asked Arthur to join Sears. General Wood was a family friend but not a relative.

Pictured from left to right are Gov. Richard Ogilvie, Angus Ray, Lawrence Kimpton, and Ian MacLeod Campbell. Ray, born in Canada in 1912, was a graduate of Colgate University and moved to the United States, where he worked in the publishing business—first for R.R. Donnelly Co. and then as vice president of Haywood Publishing. (Sharon Ray.)

From left to right are Angus Ray, Hughston McBain, and British prime minister Harold MacMillan. Ray founded Angus Ray Publishing and published the *Highlander Magazine*. Circulated nationally, it is the largest publication devoted to Scottish interests. Ray was a resident of Barrington Hills. He served as president of the Illinois St. Andrew Society and was recognized as its Distinguished Citizen in 1972. (Sharon Ray.)

William Graham, seen right in 1965, earned chemistry and law degrees from the University of Chicago. He served as CEO of Baxter International for nearly 30 years. In that time, Baxter became known for several firsts, the artificial kidney, a plastic blood-collection system, and a clotting factor for hemophiliacs. Graham was the 1973 Illinois St. Andrew Society Distinguished Citizen and made his home in Kenilworth.

David Kennedy was the 1966 Illinois St. Andrew Society Distinguished Citizen. Kennedy was born in 1905 in Utah, where his parents owned a ranch. After college, he became a staffer for the Federal Reserve Board in Washington, DC. In 1946, he joined Continental Illinois Bank, where he eventually became chairman. In 1972, President Nixon appointed Kennedy secretary of the US Treasury. Kennedy made his home in Winnetka.

Daniel MacMaster was the 1978 Illinois St. Andrew Society Distinguished Citizen. MacMaster attended the University of Chicago through a work-study scholarship. MacMaster worked at the Museum of Science and Industry. Most of the museum still had dirt floors, and steel oil drums were used as stoves in the winter. He was employed by the museum for 45 years, starting as an exhibit demonstrator and retiring as president.

In this 1971 photograph are William Harrison Fetridge and Gov. Richard B. Ogilvie. In 1968, Ogilvie was the Illinois St. Andrew Society Distinguished Citizen. In 1980, Fetridge was the honoree. Fetridge was a lieutenant during World War II, and after the war he worked for *Popular Mechanics* magazine. Fetridge is one of only six men to hold all four top-tier awards from the Boy Scouts of America.

Harold Byron Smith Jr. was the 1983 Illinois St. Andrew Society Distinguished Citizen. He was born in Chicago in 1933, the great-grandson of Byron Smith, who was the founder of the Northern Trust. After Princeton, he earned his MBA from Northwestern University, where he later served as a trustee. Harold Jr. worked for Illinois Tool Works, eventually serving as president from 1972 until 1981.

Frederick Gillies Jaicks was the Illinois St. Andrew Society Distinguished Citizen in 1986. His mother's family was from Beith, Scotland, and his paternal side was also partly Scottish. Jaicks joined Inland Steel after graduating from Cornell. During World War II, he was a naval pilot stationed in Iceland, where he hunted German submarines. After the war, he returned to Inland Steel and rose to chairman of the company in 1971.

Bryan Seaborn Reid Jr. was the 1987 Illinois St. Andrew Society Distinguished Citizen. In 1949, he married Marian Vilas. Bryan Jr. was born in Chicago in 1925. He was CEO of Cherry-Burrell in Cedar Rapids and Paxall Corporation of Chicago. Reid served on the board of the Boy Scouts of America. His family made their home at 788 Woodland in Lake Forest.

Alanson and Margaret (Reid) Donald lived at 970 Verda Lane in Lake Forest. Alanson was president of Miller Oil Company of Barrington. Margaret was the daughter of Bryan Seaborn Reid, who lived at 788 Woodland Road in Lake Forest. Alanson and Margaret Donald were the parents of twin daughters Alison and April. Alanson was a Life Member of the Illinois St. Andrew Society.

Abner Kingman Douglass was born in 1896. He was a member of the Illinois St. Andrew Society and made his home in Lake Forest. He graduated from Yale in 1918. During World War I, he served as a pilot. Douglass was an investment banker and also assistant director of the CIA. In 1947, he married Adele Astaire, sister of actor Fred Astaire. (The Douglass family.)

Abner Kingman Douglass Jr. was the 1989 Illinois St. Andrew Society Distinguished Citizen. He was born in 1923, attended Yale University, and served in the Army Infantry during World War II. He was a successful investment banker and made his home on Laurel Avenue in Lake Forest. He rallied support for a constitutional convention to draft a new Illinois constitution, which was ratified in 1970.

Clayton Kirkpatrick, president of the *Chicago Tribune*, was the 1977 Illinois St. Andrew Society Distinguished Citizen. He was born in Waterman, Illinois, the son of a machine shop operator. After graduating from the University of Illinois, he joined the *Chicago Tribune* as a reporter. During World War II, he was awarded the Bronze Star. Under Kirkpatrick's leadership, the *Tribune* famously called for the resignation of President Nixon.

STANTON COOK

Stanton R. Cook was the 1985 Illinois St. Andrew Society Distinguished Citizen. Cook served as chief executive of the Tribune Company. He led a $20.5 million purchase of the Chicago Cubs and Wrigley Field. The Cook family had moved from Scotland to New Hampshire and then Illinois. Cook died in his Kenilworth home at age 90.

DISCOVER THOUSANDS OF LOCAL HISTORY BOOKS FEATURING MILLIONS OF VINTAGE IMAGES

Arcadia Publishing, the leading local history publisher in the United States, is committed to making history accessible and meaningful through publishing books that celebrate and preserve the heritage of America's people and places.

Find more books like this at
www.arcadiapublishing.com

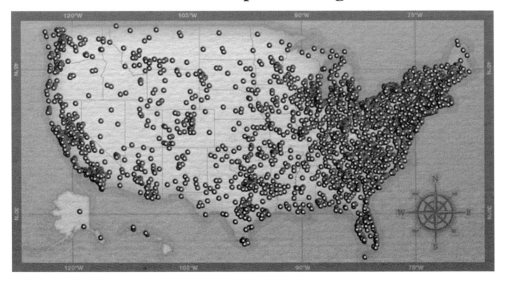

Search for your hometown history, your old stomping grounds, and even your favorite sports team.